ESSENTIAL LESSONS

for School Leaders

This book is dedicated to everyone with

whom I have worked throughout

my career who has helped

me learn these lessons

JOSEPH MURPHY

ESSENTIAL LESSONS
for School
Leaders

CORWIN
A SAGE Company

CORWIN
A SAGE Company

FOR INFORMATION:

Corwin

A SAGE Company

2455 Teller Road

Thousand Oaks, California 91320

(800) 233-9936

Fax: (800) 417-2466

www.corwin.com

SAGE Ltd.

1 Oliver's Yard

55 City Road

London EC1Y 1SP

United Kingdom

SAGE India Pvt. Ltd.

B 1/I 1 Mohan Cooperative Industrial Area

Mathura Road, New Delhi 110 044

India

SAGE Asia-Pacific Pte. Ltd.

33 Pekin Street #02-01

Far East Square

Singapore 048763

Acquisitions Editor: Hudson Perigo

Associate Editor: Allison Scott

Editorial Assistant: Lisa Whitney

Production Editor: Amy Schroller

Copy Editor: Matt Sullivan

Typesetter: C&M Digitals (P) Ltd.

Proofreader: Joyce Li

Cover Designer: Rose Storey

Graphic Designer: Rose Storey

Permissions Editor: Adele Hutchinson

Copyright © 2011 by Corwin

Printed in the United States of America

Library of Congress Cataloging-in-Publication Data

Murphy, Joseph, 1949-
Essential lessons for school leaders / Joseph F. Murphy.

p. cm.
Includes index.

ISBN 978-1-4522-0324-9 (pbk.)

1. Educational leadership. 2. School management and organization. I. Title.

LB2805.M817 2011
371.2—dc23   2011024511

This book is printed on acid-free paper.

11 12 13 14 15 10 9 8 7 6 5 4 3 2 1

About the Author

Joseph Murphy is the Frank W. Mayborn Chair and associate dean at Vanderbilt's Peabody College of Education. He has also been a faculty member at the University of Illinois and The Ohio State University, where he was the William Ray Flesher Professor of Education.

In public schools, he has served as an administrator at the school, district, and state levels. His most recent appointment was as the founding president of the Ohio Principals Leadership Academy. At the university level, he has served as department chair and associate dean.

He is past vice president of the American Educational Research Association (AERA) and was the founding chair of the Interstate School Leaders Licensure Consortium (ISLLC). He is coeditor of the AERA *Handbook on Educational Administration* (1999) and editor of the National Society for the Study of Education (NSSE) yearbook, *The Educational Leadership Challenge* (2002).

His work is in the area of school improvement, with special emphasis on leadership and policy. He has authored or coauthored nineteen books in this area and edited another twelve. His most recent authored volumes include *Understanding and Assessing the Charter School Movement* (2002), *Leadership for Literacy: Research-Based Practice, PreK–3* (2003), *Connecting Teacher Leadership and School Improvement* (2005), *Preparing School Leaders: Defining a Research and Action Agenda* (2006), *Turning Around Failing Schools: Leadership Lessons from the Organizational Sciences* (2008), *The Educator's Handbook for Understanding and Closing Achievement Gaps* (2010), and *Homelessness Comes to School* (2011).

YOU ONLY GET ONE HAND TO COUNT WITH

Educators are adept at expansion. If we can find 5 ideas, we can quickly turn them into 50 and then 500. Before long, we have shelves of binders. The problem is that no one is going to hang on to these lists. And even when a miracle occurs and someone does, no one is around to inform her or him what is really important. No one is going to pursue 16 goals or a dozen professional development ideas. No one is going to believe that 20 dimensions of anything require action. Become fluent with the one-hand rule. If you only get two fingers to count, what is important—for goals, areas of work, valued outcomes, and so forth? If you have four fingers, what makes the cut? If you start counting on your second hand, you may be in trouble. If you have to take your shoe off to count, it is likely that you have lost everyone.

LEAVE YOUR EGO IN THE CAR

Good leadership is not about you. It is about what you leave behind. When leaders with big egos leave, improvement often walks out the door with them. Good leadership does not depend on personality, certainly not on the big personality in the school.

HAVE THE COURAGE TO ADDRESS PROBLEMS DIRECTLY

I once had a colleague who told me about a problem that was vexing him at his school—a certain fifth-grade teacher who arrived to school late on a not infrequent basis. At our next meeting, I asked him if he had gained any traction on his problem. He replied that he had. In response to my inquiry, he informed me that he had sent a memo to all teachers about district policy about when teachers were to be at school and in their rooms at the start of the school day. What he told me was this: Rather than having the courage to talk to this single teacher whose behavior was inappropriate, he angered the entire rest of the faculty who were already doing the right thing. Not a wise piece of leadership.

TALK LESS

Most leaders talk too much in public meetings—and in private exchanges for that matter too. It is a bad habit that routinely dampens conversation and debate. Practice not saying anything for the first third of meetings. Pick your points of entry carefully.

MOST BARRIERS ARE SURMOUNTABLE

In the process of improvement, it is almost inevitable that significant barriers will arise. Ninety-five percent of us arrive at these seemingly insurmountable difficulties, acknowledge the impossibility of further movement, and turn back. Great leaders learn to dig trenches under barriers and find ladders to use to climb over them.

STRUCTURAL CHANGES DO NOT PREDICT SUCCESS

Principals and other school leaders are trained to solve problems and improve schools by identifying and importing structural changes to their schools— block schedules, ungraded classes, detracking, and so forth. This is problematic. The first iron law of school improvement is that structural changes never have predicted, do not now predict, and never will predict organizational success.

IT REALLY IS ALL ABOUT THE KIDS

It may seem trite to say it, but this lesson is often honored more in the breach than in practice. Keeping kids first does not negate the significance of others— but it does put things in the right order.

"This book captures all the lessons I have learned about educational leadership over the years in a simple and clear way. I have a principal on an improvement plan now, and it could have been written from this book. This truly helps me know I am on the right track."

Christopher Shaffer, Director, High School Campus
Springfield High School, OH

LET OTHERS WIN

Leaders often develop the bad habit of assuming that they need to win every skirmish, debate, point of contention, and so forth—what we call the Ty Cobb syndrome. It is not necessary and is generally tiresome. Get into the habit of letting others win.

UNDERSTAND FIRST, THEN JUDGE

Because they are generally in a hurry, leaders often judge before understanding situations. Snap assessments and quick judgments are part of the culture. It is always best to understand first.

LISTEN—LET PEOPLE FINISH TALKING

Teachers, students, and parents often have a chance to talk with the principal. Many will also tell you that they were not heard. Take the time to listen to what is being presented. Avoid jumping in with your answers until you take the time to reflect on what each person is telling you.

LEARN THE ACT OF TRIAGE

Given the complexity of schooling, it is easy to just keep adding material to the importance pile. Yet when everything is important, then nothing is important.

"Essential Lessons for School Leaders *includes brief vignettes, each one exploring a differing leadership topic. Emotion is 60% of what attracts people to a product. From the first essay forward, Joe Murphy seizes the reader's heart and mind with riveting themes."*

Richard Sorenson, Associate Professor
The University of Texas at El Paso

WRITE IT BUT DON'T SEND IT

Always avoid immediate responses to troubling e-mails. If you don't, you generally will wish that you had. You cannot withdraw e-mails. If you need a cathartic experience, reply, but do not send your response. Sleep on it. You will find yourself deleting almost all of these responses the next morning.

IT'S NOT PERSONAL

A very difficult lesson for leaders to learn—and remember—is that much of the critique that flows their way has little to do with them. It materializes not because of who they are but because of who they are in the organization. Do not personalize criticism. You will end up being unhappy and dividing faculty and parents into camps of supporters and nonsupporters.

NO ONE EVER WINS AN ARGUMENT

A little wisdom from Ayn Rand. It doesn't work for parents. It won't work for leaders. Arguments are a colossal waste of everyone's time—worse even because they often (generally) harden positions. Avoid them at all costs.

IF SOMETHING IS IMPORTANT TO SOMEONE, THEN IT IS IMPORTANT (EVEN IF IT IS OF NO IMPORTANCE TO YOU)

Principals, and other leaders, often discount the importance of things—activities, investments of time, material items, and symbols—that are not of particular importance to them. Anyone who has worked around children and adolescents should know better. If someone cares about something, then it is important. It is as simple as that, and you should act accordingly.

DIRECT THE SPOTLIGHT OF SUCCESS TOWARD OTHERS

It is only natural, when achievements are garnered and successes tallied, to wish to receive credit for those accomplishments. It is, however, much more important that others in the school—teachers, students, staff—be the ones on center stage as the story of success is told. Learn to deflect credit.

"These practical 'nuggets' of life, learning, and leadership are the real ISLLC standards."

Fenwick W. English, R. Wendell Eaves Senior Distinguished Professor of Educational Leadership, School of Education University of North Carolina at Chapel Hill

SEEK SOLUTIONS, DON'T DWELL ON PROBLEMS

One of the major truths of organizations is "that nothing so economizes effort and energy as the knowledge that nothing can be done." And few things lead to the conclusion that nothing can be done more than wallowing in problems. Leaders acknowledge problems but they move the conversation to the next level. What can we do to solve the problem, get around the problem, or use the problem as a springboard for action?

LEARN TO TELL STORIES

We live in a world where data are critical and evidence is king. But most of us don't digest information this way. People are moved to action by stories of success. Get into the habit of making your points in this form.

"Murphy has distilled and perceptively packaged a career's worth of insight, experience, and analysis into a set of guidelines for organizational and personal excellence."

James W. Guthrie, Senior Fellow
and Director of Education Policy Studies
George W. Bush Institute, Dallas TX

YOU CAN'T BUY BACK TRUST

Trust is the central ingredient in making schools work. If teachers trust the principal, the door to school improvement is open. If they do not, it is shut. You should do all in your power to develop it and all you can not to damage it. Leadership is a relational idea. Trust is at the heart of those relationships. Once it is lost, it is difficult to impossible to recover.

BE WILLING TO ABANDON STUFF

Schools accumulate a good deal of organizational sediment over time. One reform is simply layered on top of the last one. The resulting clutter can choke action. Making a school reform voyage requires as much attention to what gets abandoned as what needs to be added. Learn to jettison.

WISDOM IS NOT A BY-PRODUCT OF PROMOTION

Being promoted does not make you wiser. The possibilities for more intelligent actions that reside in new roles need to be ferreted out and learned. They don't come with the mantle of position.

"School leadership as learning is about the relationship between and among people. **Essential Lessons for Schools Leaders** *provides current and aspiring leaders with an abundance of thoughtful corollaries to guide purposeful leadership for improving the lives of students."*

Betty Burks, Deputy Superintendent of Teaching & Learning
San Antonio Independent School District, TX

GET OUT OF THE OFFICE: MOVE AROUND THE SCHOOL

Some important work can be done in the office. But it is easy to come to believe that most important work can be completed there. This is a profound error. Great leaders in schools are highly visible people. They seem to be everywhere, in the hallways, in the classrooms, at the bus station greeting youngsters, and so forth.

ASSIGNING BLAME IS NOT PRODUCTIVE WORK

Things go awry on a regular basis in organizations, sometimes due to forces beyond the control of leaders and sometimes due to human error. When they do, there is a strong inclination among leaders to find someone to blame: If only Mrs. Jeffries hadn't . . . we wouldn't have this problem. Too regularly, however, once blame is parceled out, the problem is assumed to be solved. The difficulty is that in these cases blaming substitutes for (1) understanding why things unfolded as they did and (2) taking action to ensure better performance in the future.

STAY FOCUSED ON THE BIG GOALS—THE DESTINATION

It is exceedingly easy to get pulled down into seemingly highly meaningful and highly time-consuming activities around the micro dimensions of the organization. Details are always important and often require attention. But it is the leader's job to ensure that this work is undertaken in the service of the larger purpose. Without at least one eye on the prize at all times, it is easy for everyone to put in long days and not move the organization any closer to its goals.

UNDERSTAND THE LAW OF THE PEDESTAL: EXPECT ATTACK

Two of the incontrovertible lessons from the study of leadership in the United States are as follows: First, people love to champion and extol leaders; the better the leader, the greater the acclaim and the higher the pedestal. Second, people love to pull their leaders down from these pedestals. It is wise to remember this as you see the pedestal being built. It is simply a matter of time until the same (or a similar) construction crew employs its tools to chip away at the pedestal. It's a cyclical process that in a real sense has only little to do with you, the leader. Understand "the law of the pedestal" and you will lead with some sense of equanimity. Fail to understand this reality and you will personalize these actions and likely be much disappointed—and hurt.

ATTACK ORGANIZATIONAL DRIFT: TAKE STOCK

One of the most profound problems of leaders and the institutions they shepherd is "organizational drift," the tendency to move in a non-planful manner, incrementally but cumulatively off course. We started out from Philadelphia headed to Los Angeles (our goal). At the end of the first leg of the trip, we are supposed to be in Harrisburg. But in reality, we are 30 miles to the north of Harrisburg. If leaders regularly take stock, they can correct for this drift and re-center the trip. If they don't, they will set out on the second leg of the trip in a straight line 30 miles to the north of where they should. On subsequent legs of the trip, there will be still more drift, sometimes leading back to the original pathways but often farther and farther away. Instead of ending up in the vicinity of Los Angeles, the organization is likely to end up in Seattle—doing things it shouldn't be doing. And the leader will not know why until it is too late to do much about it. Planned stocktaking will go a long way to preventing organizational drift.

ACKNOWLEDGE THE REALITY OF ORGANIZATIONAL SEDIMENT

Remember that the organization was not created the day you were handed the leadership reins. Things build up in organizations—culture, policies, norms, procedures, and so forth. Leaders do not need to be captured by this reality. Yet they need to be aware of it and lead from this knowledge.

"**Essential Lessons for School Leaders** *is a testimony to the author's deep knowledge of school cultures and his reflection on his rich and broad professional experience.*"

Jackie A. Walsh, Consultant and Author
Montgomery, AL

IT IS DIFFICULT TO LEAD WHAT YOU DON'T UNDERSTAND

Leaders sometimes find themselves put in charge of units or operations that they do not know or do not know well. For example, assistant principals at the high school level are often assigned to be elementary school principals. History teaches us that, at least at the mid-leader level, this is not a productive pathway to organizational success. Leaders who find themselves in these situations need to assume a strong learning stance. It is only with the development of some deep knowledge of the unit or operation in question that success becomes a possibility.

DO NOT BE LED ASTRAY BY THE LEADERSHIP–MANAGEMENT SOPHISTRY

Most of the leadership literature would have you believe that leadership and management are distinct entities, separated by a wide chasm. Leaders are extolled while mere managers are portrayed as competent but poor relations. This is, as anyone who has ever led an organization knows, baloney of the most misguided variety. Leadership is a simple concept. It is first about developing a firm understanding of a good place for the organization to be and second about getting everyone to move the institution in that direction. Most of the heavy leadership work unfolds in the hour-by-hour, day-by-day, week-by-week management of the organization. Great leaders almost always lead by managing exceptionally well.

DON'T CONFUSE BUSYNESS WITH PRODUCTIVITY

Most people in leadership positions are exceptionally busy people. They see themselves coming and going, from the first sip of coffee in the morning until oftentimes well into the evening. Being busy is a good thing. It provides the avenues for possible gains. But being busy is never an end. And it sometimes gets in the way of productivity. To say "I had a long day and worked exceedingly hard" always needs to be followed with this codicil: "And I moved us x number of steps closer to our goal."

THE PEOPLE WHO WROTE THE GOLDEN RULE WERE TALKING TO LEADERS TOO

Throughout the lessons we present in this book, a number of crosscutting themes emerge. Perhaps the most essential of these is the importance of the human dimension of schools. More specifically, these lessons routinely expose the centrality of relations between leaders and those they serve—students, teachers, and parents/community members. At the heart of the relationship story line is a simple but powerful leadership lesson, one that is often difficult to see in action in many schools: Leaders need to treat all those with whom they work as they themselves would like to be treated.

UNDERSTAND THE LAW OF CREDIT AND BLAME

The most insightful writers in the area of leadership concluded a long time ago that leaders get much more credit than they deserve when things go well and much more blame than they deserve when things go poorly. As a leader, "the law of credit and blame" applies to you. Remember to be somewhat humble when the laurels are being tossed your way. Equally important, do not be bruised when a healthy helping of blame is served up. And do not accept the mantle of villain too easily.

ATTEND TO THE SLOPE AND INSENSITIVITY

Leadership and sensitivity often move in opposite directions. The higher one climbs the leadership ladder, the easier it is to become insensitive to the feelings of those below, especially those two or more rungs removed. There is a natural logic to this as leaders lose contact with those they lead and reset their sights on higher organizational goals. But the process is not ordained or inevitable. Good leaders are aware of the "slope of insensitivity" and they work hard at remembering that humans are really fairly sensitive creatures. They also work hard to stay in touch with those they lead.

ACKNOWLEDGE THE FEMALE HERESY

My own observations from the last 40 years have led me to conclude that many women (certainly all of the women leaders for whom I worked and many peers) do not "lead" the way leadership is written up in the textbooks—or more precisely, from formulas crafted from studies of their male counterparts. The lesson for male leaders is, I believe, twofold as regards the "female heresy." First, they need to be careful not to measure these leaders solely in terms of prevailing paradigms. Second, they need to be careful not to try to reshape their female protégées and colleagues in a mold that may do more harm than good in developing their leadership talents.

WORK INDUCTIVELY SOMETIMES: THERE IS WISDOM DOWN BELOW

There is a predilection among many leaders to look upward for wisdom—and we might add, outside the organization as well. To be sure, these can be good repositories of knowledge. But as much if not more can be learned by, in planful ways, talking with and working with those in the organization, especially those working on the work. As a corollary, it is worth noting that it is the most profound avenue leaders have for teaching.

OPEN LEADERSHIP IS BETTER THAN CLOSED LEADERSHIP

Transparency is a popular concept. But it is often honored more in the breach than in reality by leaders. Leadership by secrecy is no more effective than leadership by intimidation. It does not foster the development of productive relationships or nurture the emergence of trust, which is at the heart of all leadership. It creates skepticism and promotes the formation of cliques. Being too open can sometimes get a leader in trouble—but is always a better kind of trouble than that which comes from secrecy.

GIVE EVERYTHING AWAY

School leaders are in a unique position to receive things: a plate of cookies from a thankful parent, a box of candy from a vendor, books from other suppliers, and so forth. These tokens of appreciation are part of the job and part of the role. Make it a rule to turn around and give every one of these gifts away to people in the school. Give the flowers to one of the staff members in the office. Take the candy and cookies to the faculty lounge with a note of thanks. Give the plush bear to a student leader.

"Joseph Murphy has distilled his life experiences into this collection of lessons that cover a broad range of topics from details of professional practice to larger philosophical perspectives on school leadership."

Daniel J. Gutchewsky, Associate Principal
Clayton High School, Clayton, MO

PLAY AT THE EDGE

Think of the organization as a circle, with safety in the middle and risk taking on the outer surface. Almost all the pressures from inside and outside the organization push leaders to the center of the circle. The problem with this is that the center is the place where new ideas, proactive endeavors, and entrepreneurial actions are almost never found. Average leaders stay in this low-productivity comfort zone. Good leaders play at the outer edge of the circle, with one foot inside and one foot outside. If you have both feet out, you will be killed off as a radical. With both feet inside, you'll end up a caretaker. Good leaders know, often intuitively, that they need to have one foot in and one foot out. They also know that it is good to be a small irritant at times.

BEWARE THE BINDER

Schools and school districts are notorious for developing thick binders of information that are expected to direct actions. They are full of information such as policies, contracts, operating procedures, and so forth. Binders have their place in running the organization. They just don't have much to do with leadership. "Managing through the binder" may keep you out of trouble, but it is not likely to make you an effective leader or help you build a highly effective organization.

MONITOR WHAT IS IMPORTANT

There is a prevailing adage in the leadership world that what gets monitored gets done. The advanced version holds that what gets monitored and informed by that action gets done. Leaders often assume that things are getting done, and being done well. Good leaders, on the other hand, are aggressive monitors. They have a set of three to five critical issues that are never far from their minds and hearts as they run their organizations. (Remember the one-hand rule.) In addition, they watch the organization all the time through a "monitoring monocle." They know there is a difference between looking and seeing.

CONTEXT ALWAYS MATTERS

No two organizations are the same. No two employees are the same. No two problems or opportunities are the same. Knowing standard ways of doing business is important. But good leaders never lose sight of the second iron law of school improvement: Context is always important. For leaders to be effective, this means following one of two paths. First, always pick situations that align with the way you lead (e.g., turnaround situations for organizations in crisis mode). Second, learn to adapt the way you lead to the prevailing context—culture, life cycle of an intervention, organizational history, needs of employers, and so forth. Since the first pathway is often not an option, wise leaders become adept at understanding organizational context and tuning their leadership accordingly.

HIRE PEOPLE BRIGHTER THAN YOURSELF

Leaders are sometimes (often) gun shy about surrounding themselves with people more gifted than they are. This is a profound leadership error. It says much about a leader's self-confidence. Good leaders understand that they are only as good as those who work for them. They also know that organizational quality will always shine on them.

"Joseph Murphy has artfully captured the essence of educational leadership through a series of essays that extrapolate the truths as well as the myths about what leadership is and is not."

Essie H. Richardson, Leadership Coach
Coaching for Results, Columbus, OH

LEARN TO MANAGE UP

Leaders often assume that their job is to take the rules of the game and the materials that are handed them and set out on the leadership voyage. This is a critical part of the leadership narrative, for sure. But to be most effective, leaders needs to understand they can "manage up" to shape the rules of the game and help determine what tools they are provided. Leaders need to be proactive in shaping the expectations and systems that expand or confine their leadership.

VALUES ARE ESSENTIAL

Data and leadership have always traveled well together. Indeed, data are essential to making good decisions. Values and leadership have traditionally enjoyed a less healthy relationship. Indeed, much work over the years has been devoted to forging out the impurities of values in the making of leaders. But we know that values are a critical component of effective leadership, both for determining the ends that are selected and in selecting the processes used to reach those goals. Leaders need to take time to understand and assess their values. And they need to work on supplementing their portfolios when they discern missing or poorly developed values.

MENTOR ALL THE TIME

Good leaders are strong mentors. They consciously work to help others learn the art, craft, and science of leading. It is part of the DNA of good leaders, not simply a set of actions they turn on when someone is assigned to them to mentor. Good leaders keep their eyes open all the time for opportunities to impart the lessons of leadership. And because these messages may not be intuitively obvious, they take the time to explain the moves they make.

ACTIONS RULE

Modeling through actions is by far the most powerful way for managers to lead and to convey the underlying values of the organization. Leaders can write until their fingers fall off. They can talk until their tongues fall out. But they need to remember it is what they do that will most influence people. If you are trying to convince staff of the need to reach out to extend time for students placed at risk, then taking 45 minutes a week to tutor a youngster after school will convey more to teachers than the best written plan. If you are working to get students to take ownership for their physical environment, stopping to pick up trash on the floor will have more effect than all the posters you can paste in the halls.

CONFRONT PROBLEMS

Organizational scholars and leadership analysts help us see a key difference between less and more effective leaders. When troubles come, poor leaders allow their organizations to focus on responses that confound those troubles: ignoring the problem, withdrawal, blaming, denial, reinterpreting the problem, defending the current state of affairs, providing justification for the failure, and concealing the trouble. Good leaders force themselves and their colleagues to confront problems.

EXAMINE YOURSELF

The advice has been around from the time of the ancient Greek philosophers. It applies to us all. But it has special significance for leaders. It is not difficult for leaders to end up becoming persons that they don't know—and that others don't recognize either. It doesn't happen overnight. It is a slow and steady, and often after a certain point, inexorable process. Leaders lose sight of who they are and what they stand for. The only certain way to address this tendency to drift is to routinely examine one's own leadership. Avoid the inclination to justify actions and explain away problems. Develop a critical lens. Commit to 10 minutes of reflection every night on the way home. Use a common protocol each time. Put what you learn into play in your organization.

CARING COUNTS A LOT

Leaders who use others as ends will almost never be as successful as those who promote an ethic of care in the organization. People work hard for leaders they respect. And they are more likely to respect leaders who care about them as workers and people and who create an organization that embodies that sense of care.

"In **Essential Lessons for School Leaders***, Murphy shares powerful insights from his extensive work with educators across the country. This book teaches important professional and personal lessons, while often making us smile."*

Karen Peterson, Director, Induction/Mentoring Partnerships
Governors State University, University Park, IL

CREATE YOUR OWN FUTURE: BE PROACTIVE

Many leaders find themselves thrown into the river of management and pretty much directed by the tides and eddies they encounter. Good leaders take charge of their work and their careers. They take the time to determine where the organization needs to be and how they propose to get there. They experience the same turbulence and buffeting about as do other leaders, but they don't let it control them.

LEAD FROM THE CENTER

Organizational charts always show leaders at the top of the food chain. Sometimes it is a big food chain, for example, a superintendent of a school district. Sometimes it is a smaller food chain, for example, a department chair in the English department. But the top-of-the-chain logic is always the same. Leaders generally are taught and therefore operate as if this is the best way to think about leadership. Good leaders know better. The best leaders understand that they need to lead from the center of a web—a web of relationships, not a chain of authority. In this model, they know that their actions produce much deeper effects as they spread outward. They know that this is a much more effective way to get things accomplished than trying to have things cascade down the organizational chart.

DON'T BE A MARTYR #1: REMEMBER YOUR FAMILY

When all is said and done and you are not leading the organization anymore, you'll still have a spouse and children. It would be nice if they were still in your life and still knew you. This will not be the case if you become a martyr for the organization. There are indeed times when nearly 100% of your energy will need to be invested in the organization. But if this becomes the norm, you will likely pay a heavy price for it on the family front.

IT IS BETTER TO DIRECT THAN STAR IN THE PRODUCTION

Contrary to popular belief and prevailing myths, good leaders are more concerned with getting the organizational stage set and helping others act well than they are with being the leading man or lady. To be sure, success is dependent on the leader. But when the question is asked, "How were we able to be successful?" you want the recognition and acclaim to be distributed widely throughout the organization, not directed primarily at the leader.

"Joe Murphy's latest book is another masterful compilation of common sense, research knowledge, and leadership wisdom."

William K. Poston Jr., Professor Emeritus
Iowa State University, Johnston, IA

YOU CAN'T BURY MISTAKES

In the face of nearly universal evidence that it does not work, many leaders act as if they can undo mistakes, missteps, and errors of judgment by denying them, throwing up smokescreens, or burying them. Evidence consistently confirms the futility of these cherished strategies. They almost never work. And they generally compound the initial mistake. This is the case because the following observation nearly rises to the level of a law in organizations: Bodies don't stay buried. Leaders need to develop the courage to accept their mistakes. It will always be a lot less painful than other strategies.

IT IS WHAT YOU LEAVE BEHIND THAT COUNTS

Most of us do not think about it that often, but we will all leave the unit or system we are leading. The question of how things look now is not unimportant. But there are more important questions: What is the legacy of leadership? How will the organization look in 5 to 10 years? Have the valued elements become deeply ingrained? For too many leaders, the good they created walks out the door when they leave. Good leaders focus on deep change. They leave the organization permanently improved.

PAST IS PRELUDE

The third iron law of school improvement is that the best predictor of future performance is past performance. The leadership lessons for managers are abundantly clear. Two stand out. Surround yourself with successful people. Allocate work to those with a track record of success.

MISTAKES CAN BE ILLUMINATING

Leaders, like all humans, make mistakes. Many leaders, however, compound these missteps. They act as if mistakes were not normal. They treat mistakes as things to be explained away or buried. Good leaders see mistakes differently. While not condoning repeated errors, they clearly understand that mistakes can teach one a great deal. They see missteps as learning opportunities, pathways to improvement. Poor leaders learn nothing from their own errors or the missteps of others—and they fail to help others learn from their mistakes.

PREVENTION OF PROBLEMS TRUMPS REMEDIATION OF PROBLEMS

Throughout these pages, we have already touched on three of the iron laws of school improvement that provide powerful lessons for leaders: structural change does not equal performance, context is always important, and past is prelude. Here we introduce the fourth law: Prevention of problems is always a wiser strategy than dealing with them when they emerge. And the corollary is that early intervention always trumps later intervention. Good leaders don't put off tough decisions until a crisis is at hand.

DON'T BE A MARTYR #2: DEVELOP A PERSONAL BRAKE

Running full out till one implodes is not a good way to lead. Leaders need to develop a personal brake, and they need to learn how and when to use it. Without this tool and knowledge, one of two things often happens. The leader burns out, in which case he or she is of little use to the organization. Or the leader begins to resent this personal sacrifice—and takes it out on the very people he or she is supposed to be helping reach important goals. Developing a sense of balance is essential for leaders.

DON'T HOLD GRUDGES

Developing a grudge in response to some insult or slight may give the leader some satisfaction in the short run. But it will get in the way of moving the organization forward. Grudges are toxic to the process of getting work done. They convey a less-than-desirable message to everyone else in the organization. Because reaching goals trumps feelings, leaders need to be extraordinarily generous in overlooking and/or forgiving actual or perceived insults.

YOU CAN DO WITHOUT CYNICISM

Cynicism often plays well in the movies and novels. It is a poor ingredient in the leadership stew, however. It almost always hinders educators rather than helps them lead. It carries the seed of inaction, often destruction. It provides a platform for why little or nothing can be accomplished. It may be cute, but it's not leadership.

". . . Current and appropriate for education leaders in the 21st century!"

Gayle M. Cicero, Coordinator of School Counseling
Northcentral University, Pasadena, MD

PRACTICE SAYING YES

Over time, most school leaders develop a strong propensity to say no. Overwhelmed with input and subject to what appear to be constraints on every front—resources, policies, contracts, culture, history, and so forth—"no" becomes a central word in the vocabulary of leaders. It is also quite often the most cautious and safest response. Leaders can get into trouble much more quickly when they take actions than when they allow the status quo to run its course. But leaders in good schools and districts are adept at finding their way to yes. They understand that it is usually only through new actions and efforts that programs can be achieved. Keep a list of the requests that come your way. Don't begin with "no." Tell people you need to mull things over and that you will get back to them. Work to see why opening doors trumps closing them.

INTERNALIZE THE 30% VISION RULE

I run up against leaders all the time who are just beside themselves that people haven't internalized the school or district mission and goals. They are simply perplexed that information that was written down and talked about at various meetings has not penetrated very deeply. My colleagues need to remember the "30% vision rule": When the leader is so tired of hearing about and seeing the mission and goals that she or he wants to jump overboard, that is the point where only about 30% of the rest of the organization is familiar with them. Connections to the other 70% lie ahead, not in critiques of their obtuseness. You cannot over-communicate about goals. They need to be talked about all the time. They need to be in almost every written communication. They need to be Item #1 on every agenda. And they need to be visible everywhere in the school and district.

AVOID THE ALLURE OF AGREEABLENESS

(or Keep Your Adversaries on Your Hip)

It is only human nature to wish to consort with those who like you, agree with your opinions, and support your plans—and actually enjoy your company. Leaders are not exempt from the pull of this gravitational force. But they need to guard against "the allure of agreeableness." Good leaders make conscious efforts to check regularly with those who usually do not agree with them—the critics, the skeptics, and the unhappy. Other leaders who don't end up with a really skewed understanding of their schools.

FORGIVENESS STARTS AT THE TOP

Leaders need to understand that leading is not simply managing a procession of the happy and contented. And they need to understand that the unhappy and malcontented have a habit of saying not nice things about and doing not nice thing to leaders. Quite often these are hurtful actions. And, not surprisingly, they often have the intended effect. But leaders are in no position to dwell on these injuries. Good leaders are slow to internalize and quick to forgive.

CAPTURE SHORT-TERM WINS

Chroniclers who cobble together narratives of strong leaders help us see that they are masters of beginning with the end in mind, that they are tenaciously clear about desired goals and assiduous in planning to achieve those objectives. But they also illuminate another theme. Effective leaders are also masters at "chunking" work into manageable units so that ongoing victories are secured. They are especially adept at this during the early stages of the voyage. They ensure short-term wins accumulate to undermine skepticism and doubt and to nurture a sense of possibility. They don't simply ask everyone to engage for the long haul and await the time when the final prize is secured. They actively structure short-term accomplishments.

YOU CAN'T SAY
THANK YOU ENOUGH

Education is a low feedback business—for teachers, for staff, and for students. Because of this, good leaders are aggressive about introducing acknowledgments into the system. They faithfully adhere to the following rule: You can't say "thank you" enough. And they have a plan of action to bring the rule to life. Thank-you notes need to fly off the desk of the leader—and not all e-mails. Letters of commendation for quality work and extra commitment should flow to personnel files. Tokens of gratitude should regularly appear in mailboxes. Posters and banners acknowledging the leader's appreciation for hard work and success should line the halls. Plates of cookies and fruit with thank-you notes should be ubiquitous. Personal statements of thanks should be part of almost all conversations and laced through every meeting. The rule is to express appreciation as often as possible in as many ways as possible and to be specific about the content of the acknowledgment.

FOOD OPENS DOORS: BRING CANDY, FRUIT, AND COOKIES

There are few universals in the leadership guidebook, but this is one: Food smoothes the pathway of leadership. It sends an important message. It tells people you care about them, which, as we reported in an earlier lesson, is another proven pathway to leadership success.

"The lessons are entertaining, thoughtful, and pragmatic enough that rookie school administrators as well as seasoned veterans will find something valuable for their professional growth."

Daniel J. Gutchewsky, Associate Principal
Clayton High School, Clayton, MO

DON'T TAKE YOURSELF TOO SERIOUSLY

If you are not careful, you will find yourself in the same boat with many of your colleagues, with an overinflated sense of your own importance. Those who work around you can often feel this. It is not a solid platform for leadership. Remember that you are important but not that important. And remember that that importance has more to do with what you do for others than who you are. Try not to take yourself too seriously. And help others on your team follow the same advice.

69 GOOD LEADER'S MANTRA: FOCUS, FOCUS, FOCUS

Analysts who study school leaders and leaders themselves tell us that their lives are marked by an incredible amount of variety. Fragmentation of effort is the norm. The DNA of interactions is brevity. They are pulled and pushed hither and thither in all directions attending to a never-ending stream of highly diverse responsibilities. The problem here is that it is common in this environment for leaders to lose connection to the centrality of mission and purpose. Good school leaders, on the other hand, are remarkably adept at holding the rudder straight in these choppy waters. They rarely lose sight of the destination. They adhere to one of the critical guidelines of school improvement: Focus, focus, focus.

THE WORK IS ITS OWN REWARD

Acknowledgment of one's work is always nice. Recognition is appreciated as well. Yet effective leaders understand and act as if the reward is to be found in the work itself, not in the emoluments that accompany the work. It is from doing the work well that they draw their sense of success.

"Joe Murphy has gifted all of us with a fun read and a wonderful source of reflection."

Gene Wilhoit, Executive Director
Council of Chief State School Officers, Washington, DC

REMEMBER THE 20% LOSS RULE

Leaders often set targets with the knowledge that they will never get 100% of what they want. So instead of saying that the school will get 100% of teachers to become active members of a learning community or 100% of the students engaged with a meaningful adult mentor, they shave 20% off the target and set the goal at 80%. What they forget is "the 20% loss rule." They will always lose 20% (or something of that magnitude). So when they set the target at 80%, they will still suffer the 20% loss, but they will end up with only 60% of what they want. If they set the goal at 100%, they are almost inevitably going to lose 20%. The difference is that they end up at 80%, not at 60%.

ADHERE TO THE PRINCIPLE OF BUILDING UP

If you study leaders for a while—those in your district, historical figures, managers in industry, and so forth—you will see many managers who act as if the climb up the leadership ladder is made possible by pulling others down. You should avoid this pitfall. Effective leaders get ahead through their own efforts and on their own merits, not by running down colleagues and supervisors. Work well done provides much better footing for leadership than does bad-mouthing others.

START AS WELL AS PUT OUT FIRES

Leaders are, for good reasons, characterized as fire fighters. They are portrayed as running around, often frenetically, putting out fires in their schools and districts. They are also taught to believe that when all the fires are extinguished and calmness prevails, the organization is in good order. This is an error. Effective leaders are as adept at starting fires (e.g., creating a sense of urgency for needed action) and managing fires (e.g., keeping initiatives in play) as they are in putting out fires (e.g., squelching a problem).

FOCUS ON CANS

As we noted earlier, one of the great laws of organizations is that nothing so economizes effort and energy as the knowledge that nothing can be done. If it cannot be done, then there is little reason to marshal energy, time, and related resources in the service of school goals and objectives. Focusing on why things cannot be accomplished is a crippling impediment to leadership, both in terms of establishing meaningful ends and for getting people to move toward those ends. Effective leaders search for the "cans."

"This book takes the mystery out of sound and effective educational leadership and communicates its salient precepts in a down-to-earth, practical manner that not only imbues a leader with much-needed guidance, but greatly enhances one's opportunity for success."

William K. Poston Jr., Professor Emeritus
Iowa State University, Johnston, IA

ENJOY THE RIDE

When I was a young school leader, I had a colleague who saw the world through the lens of retirement. The really good stuff in life would begin when the job ended. My colleague died three years before he was set to retire. A tragedy for sure. But not one without a valuable lesson. The prize isn't out in some distant future. It needs to be garnered day by day, month by month, and year by year. All of the truly fine leaders whom I have known over the years have reinforced this powerful lesson.

DEVELOP A GOOD UNDERSTANDING OF CONSENSUS

Almost all the school leaders that I have worked with have a very poor understanding of "consensus." The nearly universal position is that consensus means everyone. This is profoundly wrong. Consensus is almost always some portion of the whole, not the entirety. There are three ingredients that go into the consensus mix, and they shift in weight depending on the situation: percentage of people, presence of key leaders, and depth of feeling. In some cases, if all the critical thought leaders in a school are on board, you can have consensus even if the majority of staff members does not support a certain direction or strategy. In other areas, 80% support may not be consensus if there is vehement opposition and key leaders are not on board. Good leaders do not equate consensus with unanimity. They are adept at reading the three critical elements.

ASSUME LITTLE

When I was a young leader, I entertained a group of teachers representing the staff who saw a problem and offered up a solution. Everything they said seemed reasonable, and action steps were put in place to address their concern. A week later, I was being skewered by the balance of the teachers in the school. My mistake: assuming that the small cluster of teachers actually spoke for the entire faculty—and that their desired solution was widely shared. An important lesson was etched into my rules of action guidebook: Assume little, check everything. Good leaders honor this principle in their work.

BE PERSISTENT

Most school and district work is hard; it isn't a smooth walk downhill. It is also almost a truism that people will get tired, grumpy, dispirited, and worse on the voyage— much of which is uphill and on crooked pathways. There will be points where it is clear to many if not most of the travelers that success is highly unlikely and that the trip should be suspended. It is at this point that most leaders stop. Highly effective leaders push on. They know that oftentimes the only thing that distinguishes success from failure is persistence.

FOLLOW THE GOLDILOCKS PRINCIPLE

I hear all the time that leaders need to have a thick skin; they can't let "things" affect them—get under their skin so to speak. And I have worked with and studied more than my fair share of school leaders who adhere to this maxim. The problem is that it is not accurate. Leaders can't wear their hearts and feelings on their sleeves. They cannot be so thin-skinned that they are pushed and pulled hither and thither. But having a heavily lacquered veneer hurts leaders more than it helps. Leaders need understanding. And while some of that wisdom comes via the head, much comes from empathy, the ability and willingness to feel what touches others. This doesn't occur for leaders with thick skins.

LEADERS ARE TEACHERS

All leaders teach all the time. Every act sends a message. Leaders teach by how and with whom they spend their time, and by how they talk with others. Everything matters—where they park their cars, how they dress, how they do (or don't) invite participation in meetings. Good leaders know this and are proactive in their exercise of this responsibility. Not-so-effective leaders seem oblivious to this reality. As a consequence, they fail to capitalize on all varieties of ways to help others grow and develop. Worse, they often convey messages that they wouldn't if they knew better.

"Those of us who know Joe Murphy as a national colleague will be surprised, delighted, amused, and poked into rethinking our own leadership experiences in schools and colleges. I'm glad Joe shared his wisdom with the rest of us."

Fenwick W. English, R. Wendell Eaves Senior
Distinguished Professor of Educational Leadership, School
of Education, University of North Carolina at Chapel Hill

YOU CAN'T DO IT ALONE

Many school leaders make a fundamental mistake early in their careers, and they have a devil of a time undoing it. They confuse being in charge with doing all the work. This error is only compounded by the thin formal leadership structure of many schools and districts. It is, as most school leaders learn, an especially wobbly and unsustainable leadership platform. Leaders who stand on this stage are rarely successful, or at least not successful for any length of time. Good leaders diffuse responsibility throughout the organization. They learn that it takes many pairs of hands to do the heavy lifting of school improvement.

IT IS NOT ABOUT CHARISMA

The leadership literature, and much of the apparatus in the educational workplace, perpetuates the ideal of the charismatic leader—charming, highly visible, full of dash, always on point, and somewhat noisy (in a nice way). Many act as if this is the correct frame of action for principals and superintendents, the larger-than-life head of ship. It isn't. There is nothing wrong with being charismatic, but most good leaders are not. Most are simply quietly effective.

ASK QUESTIONS ALL THE TIME

Schools and districts are complex, rapidly shifting enterprises. More so than most organizations, they are characterized by the need for a plethora of solutions to constantly surfacing problems. Because of this reality, school leaders often assume the mantle of "answer person," dispensers of solutions to all manner of organizational conundrums and personal problems. Some of this is appropriate and helpful. But too much is actually harmful. Leaders need to be equally comfortable wearing the mantle of "question person." Or more eloquently, leadership is about a pedagogy of questions. It is only in this manner that leaders provide the guidance required to help others learn to attack problems productively. It also helps leaders remember that they don't know everything.

PROTECT THOSE WHO FOLLOW YOUR LEADERSHIP

As we reported earlier, leadership is a marvelously simple concept: Find a good place for the organization to travel to and get people on board for the trip, including getting them to undertake the work to make the trip successful. This means that good leaders have lots of people following them, many walking with them hip to hip. Good leaders do not forget this. They are fiercely, though not blindly, loyal to those who put themselves out for the good of the school or district. But many other leaders are more than happy to throw team members under the bus when problems surface, accusations fly, and the clamor for accountability reaches a crescendo. In the process, they send all the wrong messages through the organization.

BEWARE THE 100% RULE OF SUCCESS

Schools are the only organizations I know in which leaders only rejoice when 100% of the people reach 100% of their goals—100% of the time. Failure has been conditioned out of the system. Unfortunately, when the potential for failure walks out the door, it takes with it risk taking, innovation, and proactiveness. Good leaders understand that when "the 100% rule of success" is in play, it is distinctly possible that little is actually being accomplished. These leaders do not expect people to hit all their targets. What they expect is for people to set ambitious goals and move close to achieving them.

CHANGING THE ORGANIZATIONAL CHART DOES NOT CHANGE THE ORGANIZATION

It is almost axiomatic that leaders in midsized districts up begin by changing the organizational structure of the district. Some boxes (roles) are combined. Others are moved. Still others are eliminated. New reporting relationships are firmed up. A new logic is imposed. All very tidy indeed. The problem here, as good leaders know either intuitively or from experience, is that such changes have almost no impact on organizational effectiveness. In reality, it is the feeblest type of leadership.

"The examples are easy to read, relevant, and would be useful for school or district-level administrators. The book could also be a useful tool to generate discussion among aspiring or practicing educational leaders."

Gayle M. Cicero, Coordinator of School
Counseling Northcentral University, Pasadena, MD

PLAY TO YOUR STRENGTHS

Leaders have two core pathways to follow in leading and in becoming better leaders. They can identify areas of weakness and labor to improve skills in those domains. Or they can deepen areas of strength. Almost everyone in education tells leaders that they should follow the first avenue. This is not inappropriate. And it can lead to enhanced leadership skills. On the other hand, this guidance did not come down the mountain with Moses. Many leaders would be better served by deepening areas of strength. A balance between the two designs is needed for sure. But most leaders in education are not in balance here. And effective leaders always play to their strengths.

SURVEY WELL FIRST

In many schools, people end up doing the wrong work, in the wrong way, with the wrong tools. This is almost always a failure of leadership. Huge amounts of capital go into all sorts of poorly planned work. Worse, in many cases, it isn't even the right domain of work. It is as if the workers are 2,000 feet down a coal shaft that need not have been drilled. Busyness overrides questions of effectiveness. Good leaders are first and foremost master surveyors. They almost always spend the time getting the drilling site correct before they get people engaged in work.

LEADERS ARE LEARNERS

Many school leaders rely almost exclusively on the portfolio of skills they brought to the job as well as those they honed in assorted roles in the early years in their careers. This is a crippling impediment to leadership. Great leaders are defined by their positive stance toward learning. First, such a perspective reminds them as well as everyone around them that they don't know everything. They don't. And when they act as if they do, they only get into trouble. Second, it conveys the message that learning for everyone is important. And where leaders fail to convey this message forcefully through their own actions, they ensure that schools and districts never reach their full potential.

LIGHT CAN BLIND
AS WELL AS ILLUMINATE

A good number of people in education work in a narrow rut where vision extends only two feet to the left and two feet to the right. Many leaders understand that if real achievements are to be gained, those people need to be brought out of the rut. They need to develop broader perspectives and new ways of doing business. Too many leaders fail to understand, however, that this process is as likely to blind people as it is to help them see newly illuminated possibilities. Leaders then become perplexed (or worse) when these people do not see what is perfectly visible to the leader. More effective leaders understand the powerful effects of bringing people into a new world of knowledge, work, and possibilities. They ensure that the transition is gradual, and successfully completed one step at a time.

IT IS ABOUT SERVICE, NOT POWER

I've had more than a few colleagues over the years that let their leadership appointments go to their heads. (See earlier lesson on leaving the ego in the car.) Worse, they came to believe that leadership was about power, getting to throw their weight around, if you will. Power is an important element in the leadership algorithm for sure. But it is not the central variable. Good leaders understand that leadership is more about service to the community in behalf of reaching valued ends than it is about power.

PARTICIPATE IN PROGRAMS FOR STAFF

It is almost a law that school and district leaders are too busy to stay with their teachers when various meetings occur, most particularly professional development activities. Or at least you would arrive at that conclusion based on their behavior. They show up at the start of these meetings, perform their ceremonial function of welcoming, and then hurry away to attend to "more important business." More effective leaders understand that this is a mistake on two fronts. First, it tells colleagues that what they are doing is less important than what the leader is doing (and almost all of the time it isn't). Second, leaders never end up learning the "stuff" that their teachers do. It puts the leader squarely behind the knowledge eight ball, always a bad place for leaders to be.

HONOR THE GIBRALTAR PRINCIPLE

As we noted previously, schools and districts are complex, rapidly moving organizations. In them, it often feels like being on a white-water raft. Earlier we advised that in this type of environment, parsimony and simplicity need to be key concepts in the management architecture of leaders. Here we add that consistency should be a central plank in that scaffolding as well. Great school leaders don't complexify issues. They also provide the kind of consistency that is critical to team members in a turbulent environment.

"The author's wisdom and wit are engaging and entertaining, causing the reader to alternate between smiling and nodding, pausing and pondering, and rereading and reflecting."

Jackie A. Walsh, Consultant and Author, Montgomery, AL

CHANGE IS NOT IMPROVEMENT

Perhaps the most critical error that school leaders make is to equate change with improvement. Most school leaders learn this inaccuracy as they move up the management food chain. Things are better here because we have a new (fill in the blank). Things are better here because we changed the way (fill in the blank). Things are better here because we saw what (fill in the blank) was doing and we copied it. Change is the sine qua non of many schools and school leaders. The problem is that there is not a strong connection between change and improvement. Good leaders know that change efforts are important, but they are never ends.

PERCEPTION IS REALITY

School leaders often live in a tightly defined, rational world. To some important degree, this is good. But there is more to organizations than rationality. Politics and feelings come to mind, for example. A critical ingredient here is people's perceptions. Leaders often engage in efforts to "change" perceptions without ever understanding them and without recognizing a core condition of life: Perceptions are reality. And there is a corollary here too: Direct attacks or "showing" people that their perceptions are "wrong"—usually with an assortment of data—are not especially effective.

OPTIMISM IS ESSENTIAL

There are a number of essential traits or characteristics that are linked to successful leaders. Earlier we discussed persistence and consistency. Here we introduce another essential characteristic: optimism. Work in schools and districts is often difficult. The pathways to success are often poorly charted. If located, they are found to be poorly marked. And they are generally rocky and often covered with brush. The trip in turn is often arduous, and success can be elusive. Pessimism can become a constant traveling companion. The single person best in position to keep spirits from flagging and commitment high is the principal or superintendent. These leaders need to convey an aura of possibility, a sense of hope. They need to be constantly upbeat about what can be accomplished. In short, they need to be unabashedly optimistic about the future—for today, for tomorrow, and for the long haul.

BEWARE THE SILVER BULLET

(or Adhere to the Pancake Rule of School Improvement)

Many school leaders are in constant quest for the silver bullet of school reform. They believe in the big event that will carry them and their school or district to the top of the mountain. Good leaders have learned otherwise. There is no magic lantern, holy grail, or silver bullet in the improvement chronicle. Good leaders understand that each well-developed intervention, program, initiative, and so forth will add only a small measure (a pancake) to the success story line. It is the ability of leaders to bring a collection of these pancakes to the table that defines a good system. And to foreshadow the future, they remember "the principle of integration" as they engage this work.

PEOPLE ONLY SPEAK FOR THEMSELVES

Leaders need to learn that most of the time when colleagues say that they are speaking for someone else, they probably aren't. Or at least they may be putting a spin on an idea or feeling that the person being spoken for might not recognize. Don't accept "speak fors" as accurate. Always follow up personally with the person being represented.

"This book reflects the powerful lessons learned by the author from his experiences as a school leader and an educator."

Essie H. Richardson, Leadership Coach
Coaching for Results, Columbus, OH

THERE ARE NO SECRETS IN ORGANIZATIONS

The following types of comments are often heard in the conversations of school leaders: "Keep this one between us." "Don't let this go any further." "Keep this under wraps." "Don't let this one get out." "No one is supposed to know about this, so keep it to yourself." What leaders need to learn is that almost nothing "stays under wraps." It is simply a matter of time before what is supposed to be secret is widely known throughout the school or district (and larger community). If you want something to remain private, keep it to yourself.

REMEMBER THE LAW OF NEGATIVE TRANSFER

(or All Negatives Come Home to Roost)

We just argued that leaders need to learn that there are no secrets in schools, everything becomes public. The only unknown is how much time the process will take. The corollary to the "lesson of secrecy" is the "law of negative transfer": All indirect negative comments you make as a leader will find their way back to the person or persons who are the object of those remarks. It is inevitable. So the wise leader will learn to scrupulously avoid conversations and public pronouncements in which criticisms of third parties are made, or implied.

MAKE YOUR BOSS LOOK GOOD

In an earlier lesson, we suggested that leaders should become adept at deflecting credit outward to students, parents, and most especially teachers. Here we provide a related lesson. Good leaders are strategic in ensuring that their bosses get a good deal of notice when things go well at the school. The adjunct is that they need to be careful not to dump on the district when things go awry, even when such critique is warranted.

BEWARE THE EXCHANGE NORM

(or Don't Buy Off Teachers)

There are a number of powerful norms in play in schools that seriously damage organizational performance. Some of the most pernicious deal with the "trade-offs" that leaders make to secure the cooperation, or the compliance, of teachers to keep the school running smoothly. The worst of these is the one in which leaders buy teachers' commitment to keep conflict in check in classrooms with instructional autonomy: "Keep things under control down there and I'll leave you alone to run your classroom as you see fit." While there are powerful explanations for why this "norm of exchange" defines the culture of most schools, leaders need to learn that it is toxic to the work of school improvement.

GUARD AGAINST THE ALLURE OF OMNISCIENCE

It is easy for leaders to fall into the trap of assuming that they know everything. Even when they don't enter this trap with alacrity (which they often do), they are often pushed into this position by nearly everyone that they work with, both inside and outside the school. Leaders assume the mantle of omniscience at great peril, however. Good leaders become adept at saying, "I do not have an answer for that one at my fingertips. Let me look into it and get back with you by (fill in the blank)."

SILENCE IS A TOOL

It is oftentimes a difficult lesson to grasp for school leaders who spend the great bulk of their days engaged in verbal exchanges, but silence is an important implement to have in one's managerial toolbox. Earlier we noted that many leaders have learned that they grasp more when they talk less. Here we add the paradoxical conclusion that it is an especially effective way to convey concern.

"What a great book. I enjoyed this so much and remember many conversations with Murphy about some of these lessons. This will be a best seller."

Jacquelyn O. Wilson, Director
Delaware Academy for School Leadership
University of Delaware, Georgetown, DE

STRIKE "I" AND "MY" FROM YOUR VOCABULARY

With the one important exception for accountability, leaders need to learn to stop using I, my, and mine when they talk about their schools. It's not your school. It's our school, our students, our work, and so forth.

"I enjoyed reading this book so much! There is such truth in Murphy's words of wisdom!"

Jan Irons Harris, Superintendent Cullman City Schools, AL

BURN THE UPS (FEDEX) RULE INTO YOUR MEMORY

Leaders are taught in development programs and learn on the job that answers to the "better schools" questions are to be found out there like merchandise in a catalog. Principals just need to find the right products (e.g., a new schedule, a better curricular program), get them boxed up, and have UPS or FedEx deliver them to their schools. Wisdom about school improvement almost never arrives in a box on the UPS truck. Good leaders have learned that the catalog approach to school improvement is bankrupt.

TEACH, DON'T DO

Leaders have a tendency to want to jump in and solve problems for others when they arise. All the forces in the organization reinforce this proclivity. Good leaders resist these forces. They learn that their role is to help others solve problems. They know that success must rest with the person with the problem, not with the principal or superintendent. Good leaders teach the tools of problem solving and provide needed supports. They don't take ownership of the problem from the learner, though.

A SCHOOL IS NOT A HOLDING COMPANY

A wise pundit once described a school as a set of independent cubicles surrounded by a common parking lot—that is, as a holding company of independent units operating their own businesses (e.g., the fourth-grade business, the chemistry business, and so forth). What makes most of us smile when we read this description is that it rings true. Most schools do look a lot like holding companies—and many leaders manage accordingly. Good school leaders have learned that the prevailing cubicle model of schools is inconsistent with organizational success. They know that schools need to be forged into communities, communities in which all adults follow a shared purpose, work together, and hold each other responsible for what happens to youngsters.

PASSION MATTERS

We have argued that school administrators need to develop traits that define great leaders. We spoke earlier about the importance of persistence and consistency and about the power of optimism. Here we note that passion is at the heart of all good leadership. Great leaders exhibit a deeper and more intense emotional drive about their schools and districts than do normal leaders. They believe in children and young people. They are convinced and they convince others that schools can do great things for these youngsters.

LEARN THE PRINCIPLE OF INTEGRATION

(or More Stuff Does Not Mean More Success)

Many school leaders believe that the amount of "stuff" going on is related to school success. The portfolio of stuff becomes a marker for effectiveness. Good leaders, on the other hand, have internalized "the principle of integration." That is, while getting goods in the portfolio is important, the key work is forging coherence and alignment among programs, interventions, and strategies. Integration of the "stuff" is essential for school success.

DON'T WOUND YOUR ENEMIES

It is not uncommon for leaders to encounter people in the organization who, for all manner of reasons, are bound and determined to undermine their leadership. Elsewhere, we suggested that "ignoring" these individuals is not a wise idea. Here we add that "wounding" them is an even worse idea. They will only become more ferocious adversaries and more tenacious in their oppositionality. They may lie low or go underground, but they don't go away. There are only two productive ways to engage this organizational reality. One, you can work with them to get them onto the team. Two, you can remove them from the organization. There are places for kindness and consideration in the leadership equation, but this is not it.

PROBLEMS DON'T DISAPPEAR

Leaders often delay dealing with problems that need attention. This is a serious mistake. Problems fester. They become bigger. They infect other dimensions of the organization. They harden, becoming less malleable to action. Good leaders have learned that it is almost always better to address problems than to wait and hope that they will go away on their own.

"The book's organization reflects a clever, relevant, and elegant structure that is enjoyable to follow and hard to put down."

William K. Poston Jr., Professor Emeritus
Iowa State University, Johnston, IA

EMPLOY A TWO-FISTED APPROACH TO IMPROVEMENT

All organizations have two essential components—a core technology or production system (learning and teaching for schools) and a culture. One of the most powerful leadership lessons from the school improvement research is as follows: Leaders need to work on both dimensions of the school to garner maximum gains. Work on either one alone will be much less effective.

RULES CHANGE:
LEARN TO BE FLEXIBLE

School leaders spend a good deal of time building systems and structures. Getting things fixed into place is important. On the other hand, organizations shift around a good deal. People come and go. Procedures and systems evolve or get scrapped. Rules change. There is a tendency among leaders, however, to hang on to old ways of doing business, or at least to complain regularly about new ways of doing things: "Who in their right mind thought this up?" "What could they possibly be thinking?" Good leaders, on the other hand, are fairly nimble. They understand the importance of flexibility. They know that game changes are part of organizations. They spend much less time bemoaning change and much more time helping their schools make essential moves to meet the shifting environment.

LEARN TO USE WHAT YOU ALREADY HAVE BETTER

(or Learn to Look in the Cupboard First)

Some leaders are regularly looking for something new to solve their problems: a new program, a new strategy, a new intervention. Good leaders look for new programs too. But they are also much more attentive to and much more adept at using what they already have more productively. They are masters at combining existing assets in new ways. The leadership lesson is to always begin by examining existing resources.

KNOW THE PEOPLE YOU LEAD

Throughout these lessons, we have argued that leadership is fundamentally a matter of relationships. We also reported that it is difficult to lead if you do not understand the business you are in. Here we extend that lesson: It is difficult to lead people that you do not know. Good leaders know (and care) about the people in the organization. They understand what motivates colleagues as well as their hopes and concerns. And they devote the time required to develop that knowledge.

DON'T CONFUSE EXCUSES AND EXPLANATIONS

In some organizations, explanations for troubles and other shortcoming often take the form of excuses. Good leaders understand that excuses explain away the need for renewed action. They work diligently to uncover reasons for less-than-hoped-for progress, but they do not allow these reasons to become barriers to renewing the struggle for the prize. They are good at organizational forensics, for sure. But while many of their colleagues see this as the end game, good leaders use explanations as a platform for further organizational growth.

HUMOR COUNTS

Earlier we reported that food is a universal lubricant.
Humor is another. It helps keep schools running. And
it keeps leaders from taking themselves too seriously.

"This is a unique and wonderful book, riddled with marvelous insights and full of uncommon wisdom. Murphy drills straight to the core of great leadership."

Terry B. Grier, Superintendent of Schools
Houston Independent School District, TX

LEARN THIS PHRASE: "SHE WILL GET OVER IT"

(or Be Your Own Boss)

This is one of the earliest leadership lessons I learned. It was taught to me by a student leader in high school. The administration wanted us to do something, and I assumed that that was the direction our leaders would move us in. I was shocked to discover that they weren't. When I got up with our president, I told him in no uncertain terms that Mrs. Wilson was going to be fairly unhappy about this. His calm response: "She will get over it." He, of course, was right. It probably was no more than a small irritant for Mrs. Wilson and was forgotten in a day. In the meantime, our organization hitched our future to the goal we wanted. The "they will get over it" rule cannot be used all the time, but it is an important instrument in the toolboxes of good leaders.

YOU CAN'T TEACH WISDOM

Good leaders understand that wisdom emerges from experience and reflection. It can't be imparted directly. Colleagues have to grow into it. Effective leaders know that they need to spend a good deal of time setting the organizational stage and arranging the organizational props so that wisdom has a chance to develop.

DEVELOP A NETWORK OF ADVISERS AND MENTORS

Schooling by its design isolates principals and superintendents. Within the organization, there are few if any peers to learn with and from. In this environment, many leaders decide to slug on alone. With few exceptions, however, almost all the good leaders I have known do not pursue that path. Rather, they create a network of colleagues outside the school or district to whom they can turn to test ideas. And they build their support systems in very planful and strategic ways.

REMEMBER TO TELL PEOPLE WHAT YOU DID

A week does not go by when I don't run up against a leader who isn't disgruntled because the good work she or he has done on behalf of someone has gone unrecognized. Oftentimes when we drill into the matter, we discover that these are not, as presumed, cases of insensitivity or absence of gratitude. What we discover is that what the leader has done is completely unknown to the other person. Good leaders are adept at closing the loop here. They not only get issues taken care of but also make it a rule to get back to the person they are working for and let him or her know what was accomplished and why. Communication really is the wonder drug of organizations.

CRITIQUE IN PRIVATE

If you have a criticism to deliver, do it in private. And don't offer it in a roundabout manner.

"This book will impress readers and become a resource they will return to for advice on how to lead successfully and avoid leadership mistakes."

Thomas Payzant, Professor of Practice and
former Boston Public School Superintendent
Harvard Graduate School of Education

INVEST IN PEOPLE, NOT THINGS

Lest leaders forget, schools are primarily people organizations. Eighty percent or more of the budget is for the people who make (or fail to make) the system viable. The leadership lesson here is clear: The pathway to better schools is good people. Human capital rules. The corollary is that leaders need to emphasize investments in people. And the subcorollary is that even when you invest in "things," the "things" are not replacements for people but tools to help them do their jobs more productively.

LOOK AT EVERYTHING WITH THE EYES OF A STUDENT

The general leadership literature is replete with evidence that effective organizations are customer focused. It is also evident in this research that leaders are the key to developing and maintaining that focus. In schools, on the other hand, customer focus is generally not a center-stage idea. And the student voice in particular is conspicuous by its absence. The norm is to think about students as raw material to be worked on. An important leadership lesson emerges here: Learn to look at how things unfold in schools with the eyes of a student. You will be surprised at how things seem—and how much you learn.

"Readers may recognize many leaders they have encountered, making this a perfect gift for leaders both inside and outside of the schoolhouse."

Karen Peterson, Director, Induction/Mentoring Partnerships
Governors State University, University Park, IL

YOU GAIN POWER BY GIVING IT AWAY

This is a difficult lesson for leaders to learn and a more difficult lesson to practice. Many leaders adhere to the vault model of power, the belief that there is a fixed amount of power and that the wise thing to do is accumulate it centrally and spend it as you need things (e.g., extra work or commitment from teachers). The vault perspective on power goes hand in hand with the "exchange" model of leadership. Good leaders act differently. They understand that capacity and capital can much more effectively be created by empowering others.

MAINTAIN A HORIZON PERSPECTIVE

One of the most powerful lessons my mentors have taught me over the years is that the best leaders keep their eyes on the horizon—and the best of them can see over the horizon. They are routinely scanning to see what the future is likely to bring so that they can build on, overcome, or adapt to these realities. By attending to this scanning work, they become pretty good at seeing the future. In many other situations I've been in, the leaders were so busy watching current operations that they allowed the school or district to be run over by the future. The lesson is straightforward: Keep an eye on the horizon.

ANTICIPATE NEGATIVE CONSEQUENCES

Most leaders are pretty good at getting their heads around the "good stuff" that they expect will accompany new policies, programs, strategies, interventions, and so forth. The best leaders, however, are also effective in discerning what negative baggage is likely to hop a ride on the "new program" train. Since it is a thousand times preferable to deal with potential negative consequences before they materialize than after they appear, the leadership lesson is as follows: Always think through the negative (as well as the positive) potential consequences of proposed changes.

REMEMBER THE THREE-DIMENSIONAL LAW OF ATTACK

Strong leaders understand that to successfully move a school or district, they need a battle plan that emphasizes three lines of attack. They understand that they need to use the power at the top of the organization and have it cascade downward (e.g., new policies). They know they must engage in a lateral manner (e.g., a community of practice for principals in a feeder school zone). And they realize that they need to push upward from the bottom (e.g., an action research project led by teachers at the school). Any individual line of attack is likely to be ineffective. But good leaders have learned that magic can happen when they engage all three.

SUCCESS IS FRAGILE

Good leaders know this to be true and act accordingly. They have learned that success is more like a flower than a building. It requires regular attention, and they ensure that it is provided. Many other leaders have never learned this lesson. And they are routinely frustrated when hard-earned gains vanish.

MARK SUCCESS BY HOW MUCH YOU ACCOMPLISH ON THE BAD DAYS

Benchmark against what you are able to accomplish on the really tough days, when everything seems to push you away from your objectives and plans. If you can do well here, you will almost inevitably do well overall.

"I found Murphy's book to be one of the best and most practical sources of wisdom on leadership I have ever read."

Tom Burnham, State Superintendent of Education
Mississippi Department of Education

EVERYONE STARTS WITH A CLEAN SLATE

Many leaders who enter new situations fall into the trap of forming judgments about people based on old evidence and secondhand reports from their predecessors. Good leaders start with the assumption of competence and commitment. People are given the chance to demonstrate whether the assumption holds. They may earn an exit ticket from the bus, but they are not denied a seat at the start because of the previous leader's opinion.

LEARN TO COMPLAIN APPROPRIATELY

If I could have a dollar for every time I have been in a conversation with a leader who is complaining about something to people who have absolutely no ability to address the complaint, I would be wealthy. Some of this is cathartic and of no harm. But a good deal of it actually damages the fabric of the school or district. It infests the culture—and "the law of negative transfer" tells us that these complaints will wind their way through the organization. Leaders need to learn that complaints need to be directed to people who not only listen but can also address the problem.

FLUSH OUT SLACKERS

(or Don't Battle Underground)

In many schools and districts, there is ample room for uninvested and unproductive people to hide. Actually, we often create hiding places for these people. The best leaders are moved to address this problem. But they have learned that it is much easier to engage the matter when these people are pulled out of their burrows and exposed to the glare of colleagues and stakeholders.

DON'T BE TOO LIBERAL WITH ADVICE

There is a fine line between providing advice and condescending—a line defined by the person on the receiving end, not the leader. Many leaders are somewhat obtuse in this regard. Good leaders read the advice narrative more accurately. To begin with, they realize that such a line exists and they are careful in the distribution of advice. Second, as we discussed already, they learn to lead through questions as much as answers.

IMPRINT THE LAW OF CONTINUOUS IMPROVEMENT

(or Remember That You Never Arrive)

Leaders need to practice their craft from the knowledge that the school or district should never really reach its end. More importantly, they need to teach others that the business is continuous improvement. Key milestones are reached, for sure. But new ones are being established simultaneously.

PRESSURE AND SUPPORT TOGETHER WORK BEST

So far we have laid out a number of leadership lessons that emanate from work on effective schools—for instance, work in three directions at once (top down, lateral, bottom up), employ a two-fisted fight on improvement (the core technology and the culture), and so forth. Here we add an additional lesson: Leaders must learn concomitantly to apply pressure on the organization to change and to provide needed supports. Focusing on either element alone will not be nearly as effective.

REMEMBER THE LAW OF BIDIRECTIONALITY

(or There Is No Steady State)

Leaders need to understand that there is no status quo when it comes to school performance. Your school or district is either going forward or backward. When talk turns to maintaining ground already captured, you are headed in reverse.

NURTURE PATIENCE

We have already introduced most of the critical traits that leaders need to develop: passion, consistency, persistence, integrity, flexibility, and optimism. Here we add a seventh: patience. It is difficult for experts in most fields to remember what it was like to be a novice. It is oftentimes difficult for people who know what needs to be done—and how and why and when—to let other people develop that understanding. But good leaders separate from the norm here. They know that they will not always be there to tell people what they need to do. They lead with the knowledge that others need to own issues and develop ways to tackle those issues. This requires patience in abundance at times. Good leaders keep a lot of it in the bank.

Index

CORWIN
A SAGE Company

The Corwin logo—a raven striding across an open book—represents the union of courage and learning. Corwin is committed to improving education for all learners by publishing books and other professional development resources for those serving the field of PreK–12 education. By providing practical, hands-on materials, Corwin continues to carry out the promise of its motto: **"Helping Educators Do Their Work Better."**